GERMAN MOUNTAIN TROOPS

Fayetteville Armory

An obviously posed shot of Gebirgsjäger with MG 42 and MP 40 in a winter landscape. Note snowshoes (572/1733/27a).

BRUCE QUARRIE
GERMAN MOUNTAIN TROOPS

WORLD
WAR
2
PHOTO
ALBUM

A selection of German wartime photographs
from the Bundesarchiv, Koblenz

AZTEX Corporation, Tucson, AZ

© 1980 Patrick Stephens Ltd.

Library of Congress Catalog Number 80-54252

ISBN 0-89404-039-1

Published by AZTEX Corporation

First published in 1980
Patrick Stephens, Ltd.
Bar Hill, Cambridge
England, CB3 8EL

AZTEX Corporation
Tucson, Arizona 85703

Printed in the United States of America

CONTENTS

Acknowledgements
The author and publisher would like to express their sincere thanks to Mrs Marianne Loenartz of the Bundesarchiv for her assistance, without which this book would have been impossible.

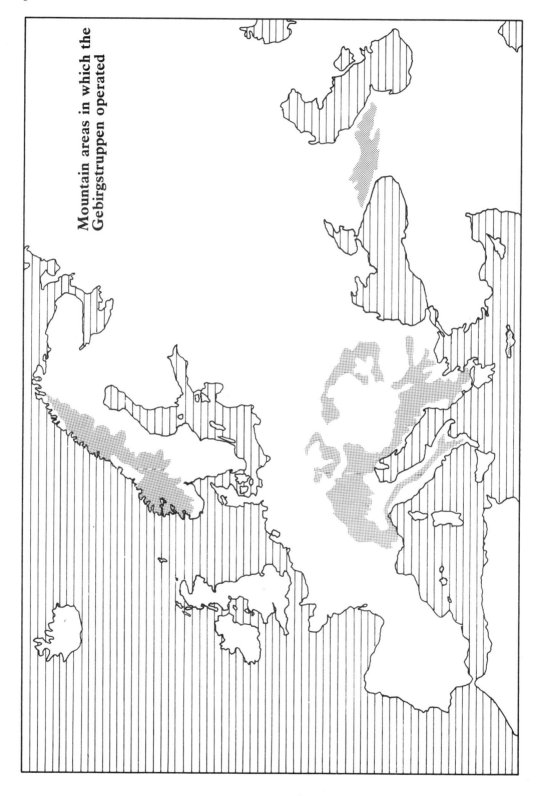

Mountain areas in which the Gebirgstruppen operated

German mountain or Alpine troops – Gebirgstruppen or Gebirgsjäger – were ordinary soldiers of the Wehrmacht specially trained in such techniques as rock climbing, skiing and mountain rescue. However, like their comrades in the paratroops (Fallschirmjäger) – see No 7 in this series – they spent most of World War 2 being employed in an ordinary infantry role. It was only in certain theatres of operation, such as Norway or the Balkans, that their special talents and training were really exercised.

None the less, they were an elite within the Wehrmacht and eventually grew to a total of eight divisions, consecutively numbered from one to eight. In addition, by 1944, there were a further ten Jäger divisions whose personnel, although not identically trained or equipped, fulfilled much of the same function. The German word *Jäger*, incidentally, means 'hunter', and was originally applied to those troops in the Seven Years' and Napoleonic Wars who fulfilled a light infantry skirmishing role. By 1939, of course, such a fine distinction had all but disappeared, although the Gebirgstruppen did utilise some specially adapted weaponry suited for man-or mule-transportation through difficult terrain. For the most part, however, they operated – like the Fallschirmjäger – in an ordinary infantry role.

The composition of Gebirgsdivisionen and Jägerdivisionen was basically the same. Being light formations they lacked any large tank or self-propelled gun elements and tended to rely upon horsepower or footpower for transportation. This is not, however, to say that they lacked heavy support equipment, as the following breakdown shows.

Each division consisted of two Jäger regiments, an artillery regiment, pioneer and anti-tank battalions and reconnaissance and signals Abteilungen. Julius Ringel's famous 5th Gebirgsdivision which participated in the Cretan operation, for example, comprised Gebirgsjäger Regiments 85 and 100, Gebirgsartillerie Regiment 95 and Gebirgspionier, Panzerjäger, Aufklärungs and Nachrichtenabteilungen 95. Each division also had its own cachement area, in the latter case Bavaria but predominantly other mountainous zones in Austria and the Tyrol.

The uniforms worn by Gebirgstruppen were in most respects the same as those of other branches of the German army, but with certain peculiarities. In particular, all ranks wore the Bergmütze, a cap similar in appearance to the Einheitsfeldmütze but with a shorter peak. From October 1942 silver piping was ordered to be carried around the crown of officers' caps (gold for Generals), but photographic evidence shows the old, unpiped caps still being worn substantially later. In addition, Gebirgstruppen almost invariably wore their proud Edelweiss badge, seen in most of the photographs in this book, on the left-hand side of their caps. Personnel of the Jäger divisions wore a similar badge in the same position, but of three oak-leaves, while those enlisted in ski battalions wore the oak-leaf badge with the addition of a ski slanting diagonally, point upwards, from ten o'clock to four o'clock.

The Gebirgstruppen wore the standard army Service Jacket for the most part, with pale green Jäger Waffenfarbe, but with the addition of a dark green oval badge on the upper right sleeve bearing an Edelweiss in white, green and yellow thread within a white twisted rope 'wreath'. Jägers wore a similar badge containing a three-branched oak-leaf spray in yellow and green upon two red acorns, wreathed in a continuous rope border, and ski troops the same with the addition of two diagonally crossed red skis, points upward.

From 1943 Gebirgstruppen were also issued with a special windjacket, constructed of the same field grey-green material as the normal Service Jacket, but double-breasted with five buttons to each row. It lacked the normal chest pockets while retaining the button-down hip ones, and had instead two vertical slanting rib pockets, as well as draw cuffs.

Invariably, anoraks were also popular, the most common being a reversible sage green/white garment with button-up hood, three button-down pockets across the chest and two pockets at the rear. Ranking on this garment took the form of the green or yellow bars and oak-leaves on black ractangular left sleeve patches also worn on camouflage clothing by other army and Luftwaffe troops.

As an alternative to the popular Bergmütze, officers could wear a Jäger version of the peaked Schirmütze with a yellow and white embroidered Edelweiss badge in between the Nazi eagle and the Reichs cockade. Similarly, those trained as mountain guides were entitled to wear a green, white and yellow Heeresbergführerabzeichen (army mountain leader badge) on their left breast pocket, a yellow and white Edelweiss upon a green oval within a white oval border bearing the above inscription in Gothic script.

It was in legwear that Gebirgstruppen really departed from regular army practice. In addition to the normal Field Service trousers there was a specially tapered version which could easily be tucked into socks or puttees, or, alternatively, 'plus fours' or ski pants. Heavy black cleated leather climbing boots with socks and/or puttees were normal footwear, and multi-pocketed sage green or field grey rucksacks with leather straps, in a wide variety of styles, were carried in place of or alongside the normal field webbing and equipment.

All these variations, more clearly shown in the photographs, make Gebirgstruppen an especially refreshing and unusual subject for modellers.

Certain special items of equipment are also worthy of note, although not all, unfortunately, can be illustrated here. Those wishing for more information, and having access to a German dictionary, can do no better than to acquire the Podzun-Verlag book *Die Deutsche Gebirgstruppe: Der Kampf der deutschen Gebirgsjäger an allen Fronten 1939–1945*, by Alex Buchner, available from specialist outlets such as W. E. Hersant of 228 Archway Road, London. Although expensive, like most of the books from this German publisher, it is well worth the money and, indeed, this title could not have been written without reference to it.

The most important special weapons available to Gebirgstruppen were mountain artillery pieces, which are described in detail in Terry Gander and Peter Chamberlain's superb book *Small Arms, Artillery and Special Weapons of the Third Reich*, the definitive work on this complex subject and from which the following notes are unashamedly taken.

There are three basic requirements which a mountain gun has to comply with in order to be successful: portability, robustness and the ability to fire high trajectory projectiles. Various firms, including Skoda, Krupp and Rheinmetall, developed mountain guns prior to World War 2, but the most successful types were the Rheinmetall 7·5 cm Gebirgsgeschütz 36 which could be broken down into several component parts for transport by pack animal; and the Böhler 10·5 cm Gebirgshaubitze 40. Various other designs were tried and used in varying quantities, including many obsolete weapons of Italian, Yugoslavian, Russian and other origins, some dating back to World War 1, but these two guns provided the mainstay.

In mountainous terrain, Gebirgstruppen obviously also made wide use of mortars, the principal examples of which have been described in earlier titles in this series. In other directions they made use of standard German army equipment, with the exception of the 2 cm Gebirgsflak 38 anti-aircraft gun, which, in addition to its specially lightened carriage, was available to mountain units in a variant which permitted its use against ground targets with the operator lying prone – a most useful weapon. Worthy only of marginal note in this context is the Eismine 42, a flask-shaped anti-personnel mine designed specifically for embedding in ice which would itself act like shrapnel upon detonation.

More so than their comrades in the paratroops, German Gebirgstruppen were given the opportunity to exercise their special skills, particularly in Norway, Italy and the Balkans, although – like most German soldiers during this period – the majority served their sentence under fire in Russia.

The 1st, 2nd and 3rd Gebirgsdivisionen had all been formed in time to fight with distinction – the compliment comes from Allied wartime sources – during the Polish campaign, where they were deployed in the south. Advancing in three parallel columns south of Tarnov to begin with, they accomplished a successful encirclement around the Zmigrod-Krempna area east of the river Wistok, then pushed forward north of the Dukla Pass to Sanok, on the west bank of the river San, where a series of sharp engagements gave them access through the hilly countryside leading through Sambor on to Lemberg.

During 1940 the Gebirgstruppen were inevitably involved in the Norwegian campaign, as this was just the type of terrain for which mountain troops are trained. Here, the 2nd Division embarked from Aalborg in Denmark to Oslo, then marched north – not without action – to Trondheim, where they linked up with their 138th Regiment which had been despatched by sea to the same objective. After establishing a perimeter around this vital area, 2nd and 3rd Gebirgsdivisionen embarked on the long overland haul towards Narvik, being engaged in further fierce fighting at Snaasa, Grong, Smalaasen, Trofors, Mosjöen, Eisfjord, Hemnes, Stien, Rognan and Finneid. Meanwhile, Gebirgsjägerregiment 139 from the 3rd Division had been embarked by sea towards the same objective, and between them the two divisions succeeded – bloodily – in helping to secure the vital west coast of the country. However, casualties were heavy and the ground extremely difficult going in places, so although this campaign tends to be neglected as a 'sideshow' in most history books, the endurance of the German mountain troops does deserve special mention.

The 1st Division was embroiled in the more temperate south during the invasion of France and the Low Countries in May/June of the same year. From its start line at Bad Neuenahr, to the north-west of Koblenz (whence the photographs in this book came), the division pushed through the Eifel towards Luxembourg and Belgium. The division was unmotorised, its heavy equipment being transported by horse or pack mule.

The division's first engagement came at the historic battlefield of Rocroi, but a more significant battle occurred two days later on May 17 at St Michel, where the division caused the surrender of a French Hotchkiss tank regiment. It pressed on past St Gobain to the Aisne-Oise Canal, a vital part of the French Weygand Line, and crossed in assault boats after a preliminary artillery bombardment on the morning of June 5. Von Reichenau's VI Army, of which 1st Gebirgsdivision formed part, effected a breakthrough on the 8th and three days later the division reached the River Marne, where it fought another sharp engagement at Château Thierry. Beyond this point French resistance grew weaker and even less co-ordinated, and the division pressed on east of Paris to cross the Seine at Bray, the Loire at Gien and reached the Cher between Vierzon and Bourges on the 20th. The French sued for an armistice on the 22nd and the campaign was over.

The next operation in which the Gebirgstruppen became involved was pulling Mussolini's chestnuts out of the fire in the Balkans. The Italian dictator had decided to carve out an empire for himself and had grandiose dreams of re-creating the Roman Empire of history, but unfortunately for him Italian weapons, tactics, morale and leadership were lacking. Realistically, Hitler should have left him to it, and his Balkan and North African rescue operations do smack somewhat of oneupmanship. Be that as it may, in the Balkans the Gebirgstruppen were in their natural element.

The principal forces involved were the 5th and 6th Gebirgsdivisionen, which were initially transported by rail to Bulgaria and then assigned part of the sector between the Yugoslav border and the River Struma, facing the Metaxas Line. This was high country, and largely overlaid with snow in April 1941. The Greeks had prepared numerous bunkers in the rugged terrain, each of which had to be taken out individually, and the Gebirgspionier detachments featured prominently in operations to remove them. It was also in this type of terrain that the pack mules – which had been so slow in France that eventually 1st Gebirgsdivision had been left behind the general VI Army advance – really came into their own, allowing the German mountain troops to move faster and with heavier gear than other formations.

Pressing through the Mextaxas Line southward into Greece, the two divisions advanced separately to begin with but then 'linked hands' and thereafter progressed together until the Cretan operation. Bypassing Salonika, they took time off to climb Mount Olympus (2,918 metres/9,573 feet) on April 15, fought a battle for the passage of the River Pinios north of Larissa, headed through the Furka Pass towards Thermopylae, another historic battleground where they were opposed, then past Thebes to Athens.

Following the fall of Greece, a large number of Empire troops were evacuated to Crete and, as noted earlier, the 5th Gebirgsdivision played a major role in the fighting for this island. (Further details and photographs appear in No 7 in this series, *German Paratroops in the Med.*)

While their comrades of the 5th and 6th

Divisions were embroiled in the Balkans, the 1st and 4th had been assigned to the imminent invasion of the Soviet Union, which took place in June 1941. Here, they took part in some of the most vicious fighting on the southern front, while the 2nd and 3rd Gebirgsdivisionen were assigned to the bleak inhospitality of the Arctic tundra on the northern (Finnish) front.

The fighting in Russia was like nowhere else during the entire war and, once again, the Gebirgstruppen were on foot for the most part, robbing their achievements of the glamour attached to the Panzer and Panzer-Grenadier boys. In the south in particular they fought as ordinary infantry, although in the north their Alpine techniques and experience did prove useful albeit, in the end ineffectual, for the intended capture of Murmansk – destination of the English and later Anglo-American convoys – never materialised.

Here, the men of the 2nd and 3rd Divisions suffered bleak, barren terrain; rocky and ice-covered except during the short Arctic summer, crossed by freezing streams and rivers, and totally inhospitable to human life. This – again – largely neglected campaign is covered in depth in Paul Carell's superb book *Hitler's War on Russia*, which I can recommend to all. Sixth Division was assigned to this front after the fall of Greece, and Carell recounts their arrival (*Volume 1: Hitler Moves East*; George G. Harrap and Co Ltd, 1964 or Corgi Books, 1966):

'The howling gale drowned the men's curses and carried them away into nothingness. Visibility was barely ten paces . . .

'In long single file they were trudging through the powdered snow, which did not get compressed under their boots, but slipped away like flour, offering no footholds.

'First Lieutenant Eichhorn was now able to make out the outlines of the bridge over the Petsamojoki . . .

'A column was coming over from the far side. Men heavily wrapped up. Most of them had beards.

' "Who are you?" they called . . .

' "6th Mountain Division – come to relieve you . . ."

' "Haven't you come from Greece?"

' "Yes."

' "God, what a swap . . ." '

What a swap indeed! From the warmth of Greece to the bitter chill and unending twilight of the far north. Yet all to no avail.

The Gebirgstruppen only succeeded in making minimal headway into Russian territory and, apart from minor successes, were halted on the frozen line of the Liza Fjord some 40 km west of Murmansk. The 7th Gebirgsdivision, operating to their south, made better headway over easier terrain and nearly reached the White Sea, but all in all it was casualties for nothing.

The divisions fighting with Army Group South had an easier time of things, although ten times as far to march. After crossing the River San they had three minor engagements around Lemberg before pushing on to the Stalin Line. From here the fighting became fiercer, with battles at Bar, Vinizza and Uman before they participated in a successful encirclement around Podvissokoie, then on to another around Berislov on the River Dnepr just north-west of the Crimean peninsular. From there it was a battle against hardening resistance all the way to the River Msus, where 4th Gebirgsdivision formed part of the winter 1941 defensive line whilst the 1st Division was despatched to Kharkov.

The Russian front during 1942 saw 1st and 4th Gebirgsdivisionen heavily involved in the drive on the Caucasus, behind which lay the vital oilfields so desired by Hitler that he had altered the strategic balance away from Moscow and into the south. It was here that men of Gebirgsjäger Regiment 99 scaled the heights of Mount Elbrus (5,642 m/18,510 feet), the tallest peak in the Caucasus and a great propaganda 'victory', but the other regiments in the two divisions were more productively occupied in fighting for the various passes through the mountains which would give them access to the Black Sea coast.

As history amply records, 1942 ended with the German disaster of Stalingrad and the failure of the expedition to the Caucasus oilfields. First and 4th Gebirgsdivisionen were forced to fall back, being entrapped on the Kuban peninsular (east of the narrow straits separating the mainland from the east coast of the Crimea). The 3rd Division, which had been replaced in the far north by the 6th, was involved in the long retreat following the battle of Kursk in July 1943, and ended up guarding the approach to Nikopol, on the Dnepr, while the 1st and 4th Divisions struggled back across the straits into the Crimea and thence to positions around Cherson, WNW of Odessa. In the north, 6th and 7th Gebirgsdivisionen managed essentially to hold their own although making no further progress through the tundra, while the 5th Division, which had been assigned to the Leningrad front after the fall of Crete, was transferred to Italy.

After its retreat through the Crimea, 1st Gebirgsdivision was assigned to the north of Greece, principally for antipartisan duties along the Albanian border.

As related in No 7 in this series, 5th Gebirgsdivision fought with tenancity alongside the Fallschirmjäger at Cassino, and throughout the long retreat up the boot of Italy, finally being assigned to the defence of the St Bernard Pass against those Allied troops advancing from the south of France.

The 6th and 7th Divisions were eventually withdrawn from the Finnish front back to Narvik and thence southwards through Norway where they ended the war without seeing further significant action except against Norwegian patriots.

The 3rd and 4th Divisions were caught up in the collapse of the southern Russian front and forced to retreat – not without resistance – through Rumania and Slovakia; while the 1st Division was pulled back from Greece via Yugoslavia to Austria. The 8th Division, which had principally been a home-based depot formation, was involved towards the end in the fighting around Bologna, but otherwise took no significant part in the war as a separate entity.

With the exception of the operations in Norway, the Balkans and the Caucasus, therefore, the Gebirgstruppen were forced predominantly to operate as ordinary infantry, just as were the Fallschirmjäger after the costly Cretan operation. It is thus interesting to speculate on what might have been achieved had their operations been more closely co-ordinated, particularly on the Finnish front. For it is undeniable that, had Murmansk fallen to the Germans, denying the Soviets the benefits of Lease-Lend, the war would certainly have been prolonged even if the eventual outcome remained the same. Similarly, had they been used in greater strength in the Balkans, it is feasible that the 'pro-Axis' states would not have capitulated so rapidly in 1944, giving the Russians access to south-east Europe and leading to the present Warsaw Pact. We shall never know.

The photographs in this book have been selected with care from the Bundesarchiv, Koblenz (the approximate German equivalent of the US National Archives or the British Public Records Office). Particular attention has been devoted to choosing photographs which will be fresh to the majority of readers, although it is inevitable that one or two may be familiar. Other than this, the author's prime concern has been to choose good-quality photographs which illustrate the type of detail that enthusiasts and modellers require. In certain instances quality has, to a degree, been sacrificed in order to include a particularly interesting photograph. For the most part, however, the quality speaks for itself.

The Bundesarchiv files hold some one million black and white negatives of Wehrmacht and Luftwaffe subjects, including 150,000 on the Kriegsmarine, some 20,000 glass negatives from the inter-war period and several hundred colour photographs. Sheer numbers is one of the problems which makes the compilation of a book such as this difficult. Other difficulties include the fact that, in the vast majority of cases, the negatives have not been printed so the researcher is forced to look through box after box of 35 mm contact strips – some 250 boxes containing an average of over 5,000 pictures each, plus folders containing a further 115,000 contact prints of the Waffen-SS; moreover, cataloguing and indexing the negatives is neither an easy nor a short task, with the result that, at the present time, Luftwaffe and Wehrmacht subjects as well as entirely separate theatres of operations are intermingled in the same files.

There is a simple explanation for this confusion. The Bundesarchiv photographs were taken by war correspondents attached to German military units, and the negatives were originally stored in the Reich Propaganda Ministry in Berlin. Towards the close of World War 2, all the photographs – then numbering some $3\frac{1}{2}$ million – were ordered to be destroyed. One man in the Ministry, a Herr Evers, realised that they should be preserved for posterity and, acting entirely unofficially and on his own initiative, commandeered the first available suitable transport – two refrigerated fish trucks – loaded the negatives into them, and set out for safety. Unfortunately, one of the trucks disappeared en route and, to this day, nobody knows what happened to it. The remainder were captured by the Americans and shipped to Washington, where they remained for 20 years before the majority were returned to the government of West Germany. A large number, however, still reside in Washington. Thus the Bundesarchiv files are incomplete, with infuriating gaps for any researcher. Specifically, they end in the autumn of 1944, after Arnhem, and thus record none of the drama of the closing months of the war.

The photographs are currently housed in a modern office block in Koblenz, overlooking the River Mosel. The priceless negatives are stored in the basement, and there are strict security checks on anyone seeking admission to the Bildarchiv (Photo Archive). Regrettably, and the author has been asked to stress this point, the archives are *only open to bona fide authors and publishers, and prints can only be supplied for reproduction in a book or magazine.* They CANNOT be supplied to private collectors or enthusiasts for personal use, so *please* – don't write to the Bundesarchiv or the publishers of this book asking for copy prints, because they cannot be provided. The well-equipped photo laboratory at the Bundesarchiv is only capable of handling some 80 to 100 prints per day because each is printed individually under strictly controlled conditions – another reason for the fine quality of the photographs but also a contributory factor in the above legislation.

Right Wearing anorak and heavily cleated mountain boots, a Gebirgsjäger NCO leads a mule train into the mountains, location unknown (313/1035/29).

THE PHOTOGRAPHS

Above Pre-war photograph showing Dietl (left) over coffee, brandy and cigar with Himmler (94/409/5).

Below and opposite page The occupation of Norway gave the German mountain troops plenty of opportunity to exercise their skills. After the event, internal competition was emphasised to maintain the level of training. In this sequence one sees the start of a ski race among Feldgendarmerie personnel, one picture from the event itself, and the winner (92/275/31, 91/192/24a and 92/278/29).

Left One Scandinavian custom eagerly lapped up by the German mountain troops was the sauna! (624/3061/11).

Below A portrait shot for the folks in the Fatherland, location Kirkenes, Norway (92/157/18).

Right Judging by the general appearance of the troops, this photograph shows a debriefing session, probably following a training exercise (94/435/18).

Below right A Gebirgsjäger MG 34 gunner securely ensconced behind a stone wall (94/437/29a).

Background photograph Crossing a mountain stream by means of a bridge constructed of logs (94/436/7).

Inset Gebirgsjäger on patrol alongside a Norwegian fjord (94/435/38).

Above A Gebirgsjäger artillery observation post with binocular periscope camouflaged roughly with tape (91/197/25).
Below Marksmanship practice for a Gebirgsjäger showing the correct prone firing attitude to be adopted when wearing skis (101/821/36).
Right A Gebirgsjäger NCO indulging in his hobby of sketching, somewhere on a Norwegian mountain (92/284/16).

Left Gebirgsjäger officers inspect a particularly nasty boobytrap set up in a Norwegian wood whereby the unlucky chap stepping across the fallen log would have had his future parenthood seriously impaired (94/405/17).

Below What a place for a puncture! (94/414/26).

Right This tree has obviously been chopped down specifically to provide a bridge over this Scandinavian river (692/263/34).

Below right Gebirgsjäger patrol crossing a shallow stream in Lapland (93/368/32).

Left Gebirgstruppen embark upon assault boats for an exercise in river crossing (94/428/29).

Below left The casual attitude of the leading boat's occupants as well as the billowing pennant clearly show that this is not an operation against enemy-held shores! (94/427/2).

Right Loading gear on to pack horses prior to a river crossing; note guide rope (94/401/4).

Below Improvised sledges in use by well-wrapped Gebirgstruppen in Finland (96/512/4).

The bleakness of the Murmansk front is clearly shown in these three photographs but, despite their target's proximity, the German forces never succeeded in breaking through (98/695/27, 99/744/12 and 99/750/13).

These pages and overpage top On patrol around the Russo-Finnish border, a Gebirgsjäger patrol is ambushed and forced to retire with at least one casualty (99/729/8, 7, 12, 23, 29 and 31).

Left Inspection of ski troops in Finland or northern Russia, circa 1941–42 (95/614/34).

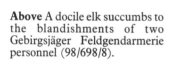

Above A docile elk succumbs to the blandishments of two Gebirgsjäger Feldgendarmerie personnel (98/698/8).

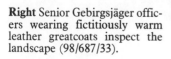

Right Senior Gebirgsjäger officers wearing fictitiously warm leather greatcoats inspect the landscape (98/687/33).

These pages and overpage The Christmas card beauty of the scenery shown in the first photograph of this sequence (left) was only an illusion, as subsequent pictures reveal (below left) the freezing mist, (right) the rudimentary shelter, (below) the loneliness of standing watch and (overpage) the problems of transport (97/647/14, 97/635/33, 97/642/33a, 97/645/23, 98/665/28a and 98/652/7a).

Above Manhandling a 7.5 cm GebG 36 through snow without the skis which were an 'optional extra' must have been a fairly exhausting task (99/719/21a).

Below left and right A command post in Finland, inside which a mountain trooper cleans and oils his rifle (99/723/12 and 724/29).

Above left The well-equipped mountain trooper. This very posed shot shows a soldier with complete climbing equipment, including ice axe, on his back; MP 40 and binoculars across his chest; crisply pressed camouflage smock; snow goggles and skis, against a typical Rhineland background. Nevertheless, a useful picture for figure modellers (572/1732/8a).

Far left, left and this page Gebirgsjäger gear: ski boots, snowshoes, crampons and an Alsatian trained to take messages. (572/1735/13, 572/1735/21, 572/1735/2, 94/434/27).

These pages and following two pages Mountain rescue. Man-handling a stretcher case down a vertical rock slope by means of lines secured from an overhead bipod and transferring the casualty to a two horse-power litter (313/1026/7, 13, 17, 22, 24 and 27, 313/1024/13 and 307/784/6).

Far left Hauptmann Arnult Abele of the 134th Jäger Regiment, 44th Jäger Division 'Hoch und Deutschmeister' (311/915/17).

Left General-leutnant Dr Friedrich Dranck, commander of the 'Hoch und Deutschmeister' Division from January 1 to April 30 1944 (311/915/21).

Below far left Gebirgsjäger General-major Ernst Baade (315/1110/13).

Below left Oberfeldwebel Heinrich Ochs of 1/Panzer Jäger Abteilung 101 (682/27/3a).

Right General de Gebirgstruppen Valin Feurstein, photographed on August 13 1944 (316/1174/6).

Below One of the men who inadvertently made this book and, indeed, this series of books, possible: a Wehrmacht PK cine cameraman attached to a Gebirgsjäger unit. PK personnel wore light grey waffenfarbe (309/843/24a).

OVERLEAF
Background photograph Pack train of 1/Hochgebirgs Bataillon 2 under the 4,040-metre heights of Dombai-Ulgen in the Caucasus (70/33/10).

Inset Gebirgsjäger encampment in the Nachar Pass of the Caucasus mountains during 1942 (70/33/6).

Left Oberstleutnant August Wittmann of 2/Gebirgs Artillerie Regiment III (708/265/16a).

Below Unusual picture of a 20 mm Flak 28 (Oerlikon) with Gebirgsjäger crew (48a/2261/29a).

Right Machine-gun position in the high Caucasus, said to have been taken overlooking the Kluchor Pass (74/106/72).

Below right Atmospheric high-altitude photo taken in the Caucasus on November 14 1942 (76/32/21).

Left Although the Bundesarchiv contains a record of PK cameramen, under normal circumstances it is impossible to identify who took which pictures. Herr Maier was one of the few who prefaced each roll of film with an identifying frame like this, chalking his name, unit, film number and date on the nearest convenient flat surface. One item he missed was location—possibly for security reasons in case a film fell into enemy hands—but this and other shots in the same sequence have been identified by the Bundesarchiv as having been taken in the Caucasus (31/2413/1a).

Below left Light half-tracks in a bleak winter landscape (Maier) (31/2406/15).

Right A damp and mud-covered Kettenrad (Maier) (31/2406/8).

Below Following the demolition of a railway bridge, Gebirgstruppen find their own way across a river (Maier) (31/2403/23).

Above Building a flimsy bridge across a river; the supporting towers have been erected and ropes strung between; now Gebirgsjäger pioneers gingerly manhandle the 'floor' into place (Maier) (31/2415/5).

Below 10.5 cm leFH 18 in the Caucasus (Maier) (31/2415/16).

Above Gebirgsjäger reinforcements disembark from an assault boat used as a ferry (Maier) (31/2413/21a).

Below Towing a trailer, a Kettenrad makes its way down a well-travelled slope (Maier) (31/2424/29).

Above left A patrol advances through the German perimeter in a Caucasian wood, the centre man carrying an MG 34 (Maier) (31/2426/18).

Left Two privates share a hunk of bread and cheese under a Zeltbahn awning (312/997/16).

Above Gebirgsjäger in camouflaged smock tries out an Italian Beretta 9 mm MP 739(i) (312/999/21a).

Right Unidentified Gebirgsjäger Oberst or Oberstleutnant wearing a warm sheepskin coat but, of greater interest, also clearly displaying the mountain troop badge 'officers for the use of' on his cap (102/868/37).

Above left A Gebirgsjäger surveyor in the mountains. Note that he wears his Edelweiss badge on the wrong side of his cap (174/1160/25).

Above The camouflage jacket worn by the foreground NCO in this photo is of particular interest as it seems to combine features of both the normal Wehrmacht camouflage smock and the four-pocket camouflaged field service jacket (309/820/11).

Left Ski troops in Italy (308/799b/28).

Right Even a ski lift as primitive as this saves a lot of energy! (313/1009/26).

Above left Oberst Schrank (right) congratulates Hauptmann Pöschl on the award of the Iron Cross, March 6 1944 (311/944/25a).

Left Two young Gebirgsjäger personnel wearing the popular windproof anorak (313/1013/34).

Above Gefreiter of a Jäger unit—note cap badge (682/29/20).

Above right Cheerful jäger with remarkable pipe! The dark areas on his cap appear to be shadows or stains, not some esoteric form of camouflage (682/31/11a).

Right Much-decorated Gebirgsjäger Oberfeldwebel with a trio of admiring Hitler Jugend youngsters (683/252a/2a).

Above Dressed in full climbing gear, two Gebirgsjäger personnel confer over a map (692/262/36).

Below left The foreground Leutnant is interesting as he wears the ski troop badge on his cap but is kitted out in a field grey double-breasted self-propelled gun crew jacket *and* bears the GFP device of the Geheime Feldpolizei (Secret Field Police) on his shoulder strap (692/274/6).

Below right Close-up of the ski troop badge (693/284/32).

Right Preparing an 8.14 cm GrW 278/1(f) mortar to fire (95/459/14).

Gebirgstruppen with 3.7 cm Pak 35/36 anti-tank gun; the Edelweiss device on the rear of the truck is worthy of note (94/446/27 and 32).

Above left In bleak conditions, a Gebirgsjäger radio operator receives a message, watched by a comrade wrapped in a Zeltbahn (94/445/22).

Above Gebirgsjäger with MG 34 (95/468/26).

Left Mountain pioneers building a wooden bridge (95/486/29).

Above right Seasonal festivities for General-Oberst Dietl and other Gebirgsjäger officers (99/715/5).

Right A Gebirgsjäger Feldwebel interrogates a Yugoslav peasant, 1943 (204/1732/31).

Left Unusual equipment for mountain troops—a barrage balloon and winch vehicle. The device on the mudguard appears to depict an elephant suspended from such a balloon! (96/506/22).

This page A Gebirgsjäger patrol comes under fire, Yugoslavia, 1944 (207/1920/14 and 22).

These pages Mountain artillery (1): four shots of 7.5 cm GebG 36s (100/781/9, 101/831/15, 102/882/12 and 26a).

Opposite page and right Mountain artillery (2): Gebirgstruppen with a 10.5 cm LG 40 recoilless gun (103/927/2, 11 and 7).

Below Mountain artillery (3): 10.5 cm howitzer drawn on a sledge (99/733/39).

These pages and overpage top Mountain artillery (4): various views of a 7.5 cm Gebk 15 oder 259(i) being transported and set up for action (312/973/2, 7 and 13; 313/1030/26, 27 and 35).

Left MG 34 gunner on the Russian front (96/544/15).

Right On patrol in the mountains of Yugoslavia. The man nearest the camera carries an MP 41 sub-machine-gun across his back. This rarely illustrated weapon was an amalgam of the MP 28/II stock and MP 40 barrel and was only produced in limited quantities (174/1159/25).

Left Keeping watch with a 20 mm Flak 38 (103/945/9).

Below The same weapon but with splinter shield, deployed in the Caucasus (309/815/40).

Right In relaxed mood, soldiers of the 5th Gebirgsjäger Division on Crete after the successful airborne invasion (166/504/14).

Below right Following the Crete operation, General Ringel awards decorations to 5th Gebirgsjäger Division personnel (166/534/20).

Above Lonely outpost for an anti-aircraft gunner beside a desolate fjord (99/743/15).

Left Oberst Dr Egon Treeck, a Gebirgsjäger battalion commander, photographed on August 18 1941 (102/899/6).

Above right General Ringel addresses 5th Gebirgsjäger Division troops after the battle for Crete (167/578/14).

Right This Gebirgsjäger Feldwebel wears his Narvik badge proudly on his left arm (99/735/29).

Above A lonely but beautiful radio outpost (307/800/11).

Below Gebirgsjäger Oberst (left) with an Oberleutnant, in a stilted situation which the Bundesarchiv records do not explain (101/812/33a).

Above Tractor used for towing cut logs for bridge-building, etc, in Russia and Scandinavia (100/768/35).

Below Transporting supplies by means of an improvised footbridge (307/759/10a).

Background photograph Harshly illuminated by a flare or searchlight, ski troops set off on a nocturnal patrol (100/785/24).

Inset Securely entrenched within a rather frosty strongpoint, a Gebirgsjäger MG 34 gunner keeps a keen lookout (99/736/4).

Above left Iron Cross citations for ski troops in Russia (84/3406/28).

Left Four-legged transport for Gebirgstruppen in Russia (100/763/27).

Above Napoleon's troops over a century earlier would have found this sort of scene familiar (163/324/10).

Right Regrettably, the note on this branch must remain a mystery, unless the letters 'Fes . .' mean something to any reader? (204/1732/18).

Above Loading up pack mules in Russia (572/1732/22a).

Left The haggard expressions tell their own story in this photo of mountain troops taken at Mikopol on January 3 1944 (708/256/27).

Above right High altitude bivouac for ski troops in Russia (572/1734/7).

Right An officer waves forward a trio of mountain troopers in a Russian snowfield (572/1733/23a).

Above left Propeller-driven airsled based on Russian aeroslan designs; a similar vehicle once held the world land speed record (622/2976/30a).

Left Men of the 28th Jäger Division in Russia, 1944 (88/3741a/11a).

Above Bread and water rations could hardly have been very sustaining in the Russian winter! (90/3912/20a).

Above right A happy moment for this Knight's Cross holder of the 28th Jäger Division as he hitches a ride on a Kettenrad (90/3909/8).

Right Despite the ill-fitting anorak and waterproof overtrousers, this jäger's MP 43 shows that he means business (90/3938/36).

Above Jäger officer looking rather sceptical over whatever this Russian youngster is telling him (90/3939/13).

Left Knight's Cross holder Hauptmann Bruno Bogert (90/3945/21).

Right Excellent photograph showing the rarely illustrated insignia of German Customs officials; shoulder straps, collar patches and armband are silver on green. This man's rank is Zollamptmann. Note that, unlike Wehrmacht practice, he wears his Edelweiss badge on his left rather than his right arm (261/1490/16).

Background photograph Landzoll personnel pause to enjoy the breathtaking mountain scenery (261/1490/26).

Inset Zollamptmann and Zollassistent of the Landzoll (261/1490/28).

Above left Unusual shot of a Gebirgsjäger trooper wearing an SS-pattern camouflaged smock (94/440/13).

Above The face of the paratrooper (Fallschirmjäger) in the centre of this photo will be familiar to readers of *World War 2 Photo Album No 7*; on the left is a 5th Gebirgs Division Leutnant (571/1716/5a).

Left Gebirgsjäger with pneumatic drill, probably drilling holes either for blasting or as anchor points for a gun mounting (313/1031/33).

Above right Even this jäger's horse wears the appropriate badge on his bridle! (90/3939/22).

Right Pause for a pipe; note that the Wehrmacht badges have been removed from the front of both these men's caps, although their outline is just visible on the original print (309/801/16a).

APPENDICES

1. Gebirgstruppen Order of Battle 1944

(The following information is taken from *German Order of Battle 1944*, introduced by Ian V. Hogg and published simultaneously in 1975 in the UK by Arms and Armour Press and in the US by Hippocrene Books.)

1st Gebirgsdivision: Commander General-major Walter Stettner, home station Garmisch; Gebirgsjäger regiments 98 and 99, artillery regiment 79, pioneer battalion 54, anti-tank Abteilung 44, reconnaissance and signals Abteilungen 54.

2nd Gebirgsdivision: Commander (?) Oberst Degen, home station Innsbruck; Gebirgsjäger regiments 136 and 137, artillery regiment 111, pioneer battalion 82, anti-tank Abteilung 47, reconnaissance and signals Abteilungen 67.

3rd Gebirgsdivision: Commander General-major Wittmann, home station Graz; Gebirgsjäger regiments 139 and 144, artillery regiment 112, pioneer battalion 83, anti-tank Abteilung 48, reconnaissance and signals Abteilungen 68.

4th Gebirgsdivision: Commander (?), home station (?); Gebirgsjäger regiments 13 and 91, artillery regiment, pioneer battalion, anti-tank, reconnaissance and signals Abteilungen 94.

5th Gebirgsdivision: Commander General-leutnant Julius Ringel, home station Salzburg, see introduction for composition.

6th Gebirgsdivision: Commander General-leutnant Christian Philipp, home station (?) Klagenfurt; Gebirgsjäger regiments 141 and 143, artillery regiment 118, pioneer battalion 91, anti-tank Abteilung 55, reconnaissance Abteilung 112 and signals Abteilung 91.

7th Gebirgsdivision: Commander General-leutnant Krakau, home station (?); Gebirgsjäger regiments 206 and 218, artillery regiment 82, pioneer, anti-tank, reconnaissance and signals Abteilungen 99.

8th Gebirgsdivision: Commander (?), home station (?); Gebirgsjäger regiments (?) 138 and 142, other formations unidentified.

2. Gebirgsartillerie data

(The following information is taken from *Small Arms, Artillery and Special Weapons of the Third Reich*, by Terry Gander and Peter Chamberlain, Macdonald and Jane's 1978.)

7·5 cm Gebirgsgeschütz 36: weight (eight loads) 715 kg/1,576 lb; range 9,250 metres/10,116 yards; weight of projectile 5·74 or 5·83 kg/12 or 13 lb; rate of fire 6 rpm.

10·5 cm Gebirgshaubitze 40: weight (four loads) approximately 2,600 kg/5,733 lb; range 12,625 metres/13,807 yards; weight of projectile 14·81 kg/32·6 lb; rate of fire 4–6 rpm.

ACHTUNG! COMPLETED YOUR COLLECTION?

Other titles in the same series

No 1 Panzers in the Desert
by Bruce Quarrie

No 2 German Bombers over England
by Bryan Philpott

No 3 Waffen-SS in Russia
by Bruce Quarrie

No 4 Fighters Defending the Reich
by Bryan Philpott

No 5 Panzers in North-West Europe
by Bruce Quarrie

No 6 German Fighters over the Med
by Bryan Philpott

No 7 German Paratroops in the Med
by Bruce Quarrie

No 8 German Bombers over Russia
by Bryan Philpott

No 9 Panzers in Russia 1941–43
by Bruce Quarrie

No 10 German Fighters over England
by Bryan Philpott

No 11 U-Boats in the Atlantic
by Paul Beaver

No 12 Panzers in Russia 1943–45
by Bruce Quarrie

No 13 German Bombers over the Med
by Bryan Philpott

No 14 German Capital Ships
by Paul Beaver

No 16 German Fighters over Russia
by Bryan Philpott

In preparation

No 17 E-Boats and Coastal Craft
by Paul Beaver

No 18 German Maritime Aircraft
by Bryan Philpott

No 19 Panzers in the Balkans and Italy
by Bruce Quarrie

No 20 German Destroyers and Escorts
by Paul Beaver

Thank you for buying this AZTEX book. We're sure you will find it informative and enjoyable. If you would like to be kept informed of the publishing dates of future titles please send your name and address to:

Announcements
Dept WWII
AZTEX Corporation
P O Box 50046
Tucson, AZ 85703